One Stick Song

Books By Sherman Alexie:

Poetry

The Business of Fancydancing
First Indian on the Moon
Old Shirts & New Skins
The Summer of Black Widows

Fiction:

The Lone Ranger and Tonto Fistfight in Heaven
Reservation Blues
Indian Killer
The Toughest Indian in the World

Limited Editions:

I Would Steal Horses
Seven Mourning Songs for the Cedar Flute I Have Yet to Learn to Play
Water Flowing Home
The Man Who Loves Salmon

One Stick Song

Sherman Alexie

Hanging Loose Press
Brooklyn, New York

Published by Hanging Loose Press, 231 Wyckoff Street, Brooklyn,
NY 11217-2208. All rights reserved. No part of this book may be
reproduced without the publisher's written permission, except for
brief quotations in reviews.

Printed in the United States of America
10 9 8 7 6 5 4 3 2

Hanging Loose Press thanks the Literature Program of the New
York State Council on the Arts for a grant in support of the publi-
cation of this book.

Cover painting by Brenda Goodman: Oil on Masonite panels/dip-
tych 16x40. Detail on cover, full painting on frontispiece
Cover design by Carole McCurdy

Acknowledgments: Some of the poems in this book first appeared
in these publications: *Hanging Loose, Long Shot, Luna, Prairie
Schooner, Semi-Dwarf Quarterly, Sic* and *Solo*. Some also appeared in
The Man Who Loves Salmon, a limited edition chapbook published
by Limberlost Press. "The Warriors" first appeared in the anthol-
ogy *Home Field: Nine Writers at Bat*, Sasquatch Books.

Library of Congress Cataloging-in-Publication Data

Alexie, Sherman
      One-stick song / Sherman Alexie.
         p. cm.
      ISBN 1-882413-77-6 — ISBN 1-882413-76-8 (pbk.)
      1. Indians of North America — Poetry. I. Title.

PS3551.L35774O53 1999
811'.54—dc21   99-058811

Produced at The Print Center, Inc. 225 Varick St.,
New York, NY 10014, a non-profit facility for liter-
ary and arts-related publications. (212) 206-8465

Contents

For my family

One Stick Song

The Unauthorized Autobiography of Me

Late summer night on the Spokane Indian Reservation. Ten Indians are playing basketball on a court barely illuminated by the streetlight above them. They will play until the brown, leather ball is invisible in the dark. They will play until an errant pass jams a finger, knocks a pair of glasses off the face, smashes a nose and draws blood. They will play until the ball bounces off the court and disappears into the shadows.

This may be all you need to know about Native American literature.

*

Thesis: I have never met a Native American. Thesis repeated: I have met thousands of Indians.

*

November 1994, Manhattan: PEN American panel on Indian Literature. N. Scott Momaday, James Welch, Gloria Miguel, Joy Harjo, me. Two or three hundred people in the audience. Mostly non-Indians, an Indian or three. Questions and answers.

"Why do you insist on calling yourselves Indian?" asks a white woman in a nice hat. "It's so demeaning."

"Listen," I say. "The word belongs to us now. We are Indians. That has nothing to do with Indians from India. We are not American Indians. We are Indians, pronounced In-din. It belongs to us. We own it and we're not going to give it back."

So much has been taken from us that we hold onto the smallest things left with all the strength we have.

*

1976: Winter on the Spokane Indian Reservation. My two cousins, S and G, have enough money for gloves. They buy them at Irene's

Grocery Store. Irene is a white woman who has lived on our reservation since the beginning of time. I have no money for gloves. My hands are bare.

We build snow fortresses on the football field. Since we are Indian boys playing, there must be a war. We stockpile snowballs. S and G build their fortress on the fifty-yard line. I build mine on the thirty-yard line. We begin our little war.

My cousins are good warriors. They throw snowballs with precision. I am bombarded, under siege, defeated quickly. My cousins bury me in the snow. My grave is shallow. If my cousins knew how to dance, they might have danced on my grave. But they know how to laugh, so they laugh. They are my cousins, meaning we are related in the Indian way. My father drank beers with their father for most of two decades, and that is enough to make us relatives. Indians gather relatives like firewood, protection against the cold. I am buried in the snow, cold, without protection. My hands are bare.

After a short celebration, my cousins exhume me. I am too cold to fight. Shivering, I walk home, anxious for warmth. I know my mother is home. She is probably sewing a quilt. She is always sewing quilts. If she sells a quilt, we have dinner. If she fails to sell a quilt, we go hungry. My mother has never failed to sell a quilt. But the threat of hunger is always there.

When I step into the house, my mother is sewing yet another quilt. She is singing a song under her breath. You might assume she is singing a highly traditional Spokane Indian song. In fact, she is singing Donna Fargo's "The Happiest Girl in the Whole USA." Improbably, this is a highly traditional Spokane Indian song. The living room is dark in the late afternoon. The house is cold. My mother is wearing her coat and shoes.

"Why don't you turn up the heat?" I ask my mother.

"No electricity," she says.

"Power went out?" I ask.

"Didn't pay the bill," she says.

I am colder. I inhale, exhale, my breath visible inside the house. I can hear a car sliding on the icy road outside. My mother is making a quilt. This quilt will pay for the electricity. Her fingers are stiff and painful from the cold. She is sewing as fast as she can.

*

On the jukebox in the bar: Hank Williams, Patsy Cline, Johnny Cash, Charlie Rich, Freddy Fender, Donna Fargo.

On the radio in the car: Creedence Clearwater Revival, Three Dog Night, Blood Sweat & Tears, Janis Joplin, early Stones, earlier Beatles.

On the stereo in the house: Glen Campbell, Roy Orbison, Johnny Horton, Loretta Lynn, "The Ballad of the Green Beret."

*

1975: Mr. Manley, the fourth grade music teacher, sets a row of musical instruments in front of us. From left to right, a flute, clarinet, French horn, trombone, trumpet, tuba, drum. We're getting our first chance to play this kind of music.

"Now," he explains, "I want all of you to line up behind the instrument you'd like to learn how to play."

Dawn, Loretta, and Karen line up behind the flute. Melissa and Michelle behind the clarinet. Lori and Willette, the French horn. All ten Indian boys line up behind the drum.

*

1970: My sister Mary is beautiful. She is fourteen years older than me. She wears short skirts and nylons because she is supposed to wear short skirts and nylons. It is expected. Her black hair is combed long, straight. Often, she sits in her favorite chair, the fake leather lounger we rescued from the dump. Holding a hand mirror, she combs her hair, applies her make-up. Much lipstick and eye shadow, no foundation. She is always leaving the house. I do not know where she goes.

I do remember sitting at her feet, rubbing my cheek against her nyloned calf, while she waited for her ride. In Montana in 1981, she died in an early morning fire. At the time, I was sleeping at a friend's house in Washington state. I was not dreaming of my sister.

*

"Sherman," says the critic, "How does the oral tradition apply to your work?"

"Well," I say, as I hold my latest book close to me, "It doesn't apply at all because I typed this. And when I'm typing, I'm really, really quiet."

*

1977: Summer. Steve and I want to attend the KISS concert in Spokane. KISS is very popular on my reservation. Gene Simmons, the bass player. Paul Stanley, lead singer and rhythm guitarist. Ace Frehley, lead guitar. Peter Criss, drums. All four hide their faces behind elaborate make-up. Simmons the devil, Stanley the lover, Frehley the space man, Criss the cat.

The songs: "Do You Love Me," "Calling Dr. Love," "Love Gun," "Makin' Love," "C'mon and Love Me."

Steve and I are too young to go on our own. His uncle and aunt, born-again Christians, decide to chaperon us. Inside the Spokane Coliseum, the four of us find seats far from the stage and the enormous speakers. Uncle and Aunt wanted to avoid the bulk of the crowd, but have landed us in the unofficial pot-smoking section. We are overwhelmed by the sweet smoke. Steve and I cover our mouths and noses with Styrofoam cups and try to breathe normally.

KISS opens their show with staged explosions, flashing red lights, a prolonged guitar solo by Frehley. Simmons spits fire. The crowd rushes the stage. All the pot smokers in our section hold lighters, tiny flames flickering, high above their heads. The songs are so familiar we know all the words. The audience sings along.

The songs: "Let Me Go, Rock 'n' Roll," "Detroit Rock City," "Rock and Roll All Nite."

The decibel level is tremendous. Steve and I can feel the sound waves crashing against the Styrofoam cups we hold over our faces. Aunt and Uncle are panicked, finally convinced that the devil plays a mean guitar. This is too much for them. It is also too much for Steve and me, but we pretend to be disappointed when Aunt and Uncle drag us out of the Coliseum.

During the drive home, Aunt and Uncle play Christian music on the radio. Loudly and badly, they sing along. Steve and I are in the back of the Pacer, looking up through the strangely curved rear window. There is a meteor shower, the largest in a decade. Steve and I smell like pot smoke. We smile at this. Our ears ring. We make wishes on the shooting stars, though both of us know that a shooting star is not a star. It's just a sliver of stone.

*

I made a very conscious decision to marry an Indian woman, who made a very conscious decision to marry me.

Our hope: to give birth to and raise Indian children who love themselves. That is the most revolutionary act.

*

1982: I am the only Indian student at Reardan High, an all-white school in a small farm town just outside my reservation. I am in the pizza parlor, sharing a deluxe with my white friends. We are talking and laughing. A drunk Indian walks in. He staggers to the counter and orders a beer. The waiter ignores him. We are all silent.

At our table, S is shaking her head. She leans toward us as if to share a secret.

"Man," she says, "I hate Indians."

*

I am curious about the writers who identify themselves as mixed-blood Indians. Is it difficult for them to decide which container they should put their nouns and verbs into? Invisibility, after all, can be useful, as a blonde, Aryan-featured Jew in Germany might have found during World War II. Then again, I think of the horror stories that such a pale undetected Jew could tell about life during the Holocaust.

*

An Incomplete List of People I Wish Were Indian

Kareem Abdul-Jabbar
Adam
Muhammad Ali
Susan B. Anthony
Jimmy Carter
Patsy Cline
D.B. Cooper
Robert DeNiro
Emily Dickinson
Isadora Duncan
Amelia Earhart
Eve
Diane Fossey
Jesus Christ
Robert Johnson
Helen Keller
Billie Jean King
Martin Luther King, Jr.
John Lennon
Mary Magdalene
Pablo Neruda
Flannery O'Connor
Rosa Parks
Wilma Rudolph

Sappho
William Shakespeare
Bruce Springsteen
Meryl Streep
John Steinbeck
Superman
Harriet Tubman
Voltaire
Walt Whitman

*

1995: Summer. Seattle, Washington. I am idling at a red light when a car filled with white boys pulls up beside me. The white boy in the front passenger seat leans out his window.

"I hate you Indian motherfuckers," he screams.

I
quietly wait for the green light.

1978: David, Randy, Steve, and I decide to form a reservation doowop group, like the Platters. During recess, we practice behind the old tribal school. Steve, a falsetto, is the best singer. I am the worst singer, but have the deepest voice, and am therefore an asset.

"What songs do you want to sing?" asks David.

"Tracks of My Tears," says Steve, who always decides these kind of things.

We sing, desperately trying to remember the lyrics to that song. We try to remember other songs. We remember the chorus to most, the first verse of a few, and only one in its entirety. For some reason, we all know the lyrics of "Monster Mash." However, I'm the only one who can manage to sing with the pseudo-Transylvanian accent that the song requires. This dubious skill makes me the lead singer, despite Steve's protests.

"We need a name for our group," says Randy.

"How about The Warriors?" I ask.

Everybody agrees. We've watched a lot of Westerns.

We sing "Monster Mash" over and over. We want to be famous. We want all the little Indian girls to shout our names. Finally, after days of practice, we are ready for our debut. Walking in line like soldiers, the four of us parade around the playground. We sing "Monster Mash." I am in front, followed by Steve, David, then Randy, who is the shortest, but the toughest fighter our reservation has ever known. We sing. We are The Warriors. All the other Indian boys and girls line up behind us as we march. We are heroes. We are loved. I sing with everything I have inside of me: pain, happiness, anger, depression, heart, soul, small intestine. I sing and am rewarded with people who listen.

That is why I am a poet.

*

I remember watching Richard Nixon, during the Watergate affair, as he held a press conference and told the entire world that he was not a crook.

For the first time, I understood that storytellers could be bad people.

*

Poetry = Anger x Imagination

*

Every time I venture into the bookstore, I find another book about Indians. There are hundreds of books about Indians published every year, yet so few are written by Indians. I gather all the books written about Indians. I discover:

A book written by a person who identifies as mixed-blood will sell more copies than a book written by a person who identifies as strictly Indian.

A book written by a non-Indian will sell more copies than a book written by either a mixed-blood or an Indian writer.

Reservation Indian writers are rarely published in any form.

A book about Indian life in the past, whether written by a non-Indian, mixed-blood, or Indian, will sell more copies than a book about Indian life in the twentieth century.

If you are a non-Indian writing about Indians, it is almost guaranteed that something positive will be written about you by Tony Hillerman.

Indian writers who are women will be compared with Louise Erdrich. Indian writers who are men will be compared with Michael Dorris.

A very small percentage of the readers of Indian literature have heard of Simon J. Ortiz. This is a crime.

Books about the Sioux sell more copies than all of the books written about other tribes combined.

Mixed-blood writers often write about any tribe which interests them, whether or not they are related to that tribe.

Writers who use obvious Indian names, such as Eagle Woman and Pretty Shield, are usually non-Indian.

Non-Indian writers usually say "Great Spirit," "Mother Earth," "Two-Legged, Four-Legged, and Winged." Mixed-blood writers usually say "Creator, "Mother Earth," "Two-Legged, Four- Legged, and Winged." Indian writers usually say "God," "Mother Earth," "Human Being, Dog, and Bird."

If a book about Indians contains no dogs, then it was written by a non-Indian or mixed-blood writer.

If on the cover of a book there are winged animals who aren't supposed to have wings, then it was written by a non-Indian.

Successful non-Indian writers are viewed as well-informed about Indian life. Successful mixed-blood writers are viewed as wonderful translators of Indian life. Successful Indian writers are viewed as traditional storytellers of Indian life.

Very few Indian and mixed-blood writers speak their tribal languages. Even fewer non-Indian writers speak their tribal languages.

Indians often write exclusively about reservation life, even if they never lived on a reservation.

Mixed-bloods often write exclusively about Indians, even if they grew up in non-Indian communities.

Non-Indian writers always write about reservation life.

Nobody has written the great urban Indian novel yet.

Most non-Indians who write about Indians are fiction writers. Fiction about Indians sells.

*

Have you stood in a crowded room where nobody looks like you? If you are white, have you stood in a room full of black people? Are you an Irish man who has strolled through the streets of Compton? If you are black, have you stood in a room full of white people? Are you an African-American man who has played the back nine at the local country club? If you are a woman, have you stood in a room full of men? Are you Sandra Day O'Connor or Ruth Ginsberg?

Since I left the reservation, almost every room I enter is filled with people who do not look like me. There are only two million Indians in this country. We could all fit into one medium-sized city. Someone should look into it.

Often, I am most alone in bookstores where I am reading from my work. I look up from the page at white faces. This is frightening.

*

There is an apple tree outside my grandmother's house on the reservation. The apples are green; my grandmother's house is green. This is the game: My siblings and I try to sneak apples from the tree. Sometimes, our friends will join our raiding expeditions. My grandmother believes green apples are poison and is simply trying to protect us from sickness. There is nothing biblical about this story.

The game has rules. We always have to raid the tree during daylight. My grandmother has bad eyes and it would be unfair to challenge her in the dark. We all have to approach the tree at the same time. Arnold, my older brother. Kim and Arlene, my younger twin sisters. We have to climb the tree to steal apples, ignoring the fruit which hangs low to the ground.

Arnold is the best apple thief on the reservation. He is chubby, but quick. He is fearless in the tree, climbing to the top for the plumpest apples. He hangs from a branch with one arm, reaches for apples with the other, and fills his pockets with his booty. I love him like crazy. My sisters are more conservative. Often they grab one apple and eat it quickly, sitting on a sturdy branch. I always like the green apples with a hint of red. While we are busy raiding the tree, we also keep an eye on our grandmother's house. She is a big woman, nearly six feet tall. At the age of seventy, she can still outrun any ten-year-old.

Arnold, of course, is always the first kid out of the tree. He hangs from a branch, drops to the ground, and screams loudly, announcing our presence to our grandmother. He runs away, leaving my sisters and me stuck in the tree. We scramble to the ground and try to escape.

"Junior," she shouts and I freeze. That's the rule. Sometimes a dozen Indian kids have been in that tree, scattering in random directions when our grandmother bursts out of the house. If she remembers your name, you are a prisoner of war. And, believe me, no matter how many kids are running away, my grandmother always remembers my name.

My grandmother died when I was fourteen years old. I miss her. I miss everybody.

"Junior," she shouts and I close my eyes in disgust. Captured again! I wait as she walks up to me. She holds out her hand and I give her the stolen apples. Then she smacks me gently on the top of my head. I am free to run then, pretending she never caught me in the first place. I try to catch up with the others. Running through the trees surrounding my grandmother's house, I shout out their names.

*

So many people claim to be Indian, speaking of an Indian grandmother, a warrior grandfather. Suppose the United States government announced that all Indians had to return to their reservation. How many of these people would not shove that Indian ancestor back into the closet?

*

My mother still makes quilts. My wife and I sleep beneath one. My brother works for our tribal casino. One sister works for our bingo hall, while the other works in the tribal finance department. Our adopted little brother, James, who is actually our second cousin, is a freshman at Reardan High School. He can run the mile in five minutes.

My father is an alcoholic. He used to leave us for weeks at a time to drink with his friends and cousins. I missed him so much I'd cry myself sick.

I could always tell when he was going to leave. He would be tense, quiet, unable to concentrate. He'd flip through magazines and television channels. He'd open the refrigerator door, study its contents, shut the door, and walk away. Five minutes later, he'd be back at the fridge, rearranging items on the shelves. I would follow him from place to place, trying to prevent his escape.

Once, he went into the bathroom, which had no windows, while I sat outside the only door and waited for him. I could not hear him inside. I knocked on the thin wood. I was five years old.

"Are you there?" I asked. "Are you still there?"

Every time he left, I ended up in the emergency room. But I always got well and he always came back. He'd walk in the door without warning. We'd forgive him.

Years later, I am giving a reading at a bookstore in Spokane, Washington. There is a large crowd. I read a story about an Indian father who leaves his family for good. He moves to a city a thousand miles away. Then he dies. It is a sad story. When I finish, a woman in the front row breaks into tears.

"What's wrong?" I ask her.

"I'm so sorry about your father," she says.

"Thank you," I say, "But that's my father sitting right next to you."

Crow Testament

1.

Cain lifts Crow, that heavy black bird
and strikes down Abel.

Damn, says Crow, I guess
this is just the beginning.

2.

The white man, disguised
as a falcon, swoops in
and yet again steals a salmon
from Crow's talons.

Damn, says Crow, if I could swim
I would have fled this country years ago.

3.

The Crow God as depicted
in all of the reliable Crow bibles
looks exactly like a Crow.

Damn, says Crow, this makes it
so much easier to worship myself.

4.

Among the ashes of Jericho,
Crow sacrifices his firstborn son.

Damn, says Crow, a million nests
are soaked with blood.

5.

When Crows fight Crows
the sky fills with beaks and talons.

Damn, says Crow, it's raining feathers.

6.

Crow flies around the reservation
and collects empty beer bottles

but they are so heavy
he can carry only one at a time.

So, one by one, he returns them
but gets only five cents a bottle.

Damn, says Crow, redemption
is not easy.

7.

Crow rides a pale horse
into a crowded powwow
but none of the Indians panic.

Damn, says Crow, I guess
they already live near the end of the world.

How it Happens

Every day for a year
three Indian men waited at that bus stop

then one morning, only two
and only two for the next year or so

then yesterday, only one
clutching a brown paper sack.

As I drove by
that last one turned away

Then this morning, briefly
I considered stopping

to ask the one what happened to the two
though of course I already knew.

Open Books

Along with the sonnets and blank verse
comes this: the gossip
about which poet is sleeping
with which poet, about who left whom

for who. Don't you know
the formalists only go to bed
with other formalists
but the free versers will screw
anybody, even the novelists.

The promiscuous poets fill the shelves
with their thin volumes, the selected
and collected lovers, the beautiful lies

occupying a line or stanza
or even the whole poem. I am
reminded of R, the poet's son,
who smiled when I told him
how much I loved his daddy's poems

especially the epic one about love and the canyon
        and the sunset, all of it
coming together as he held the hands of his wife and son
        as they all stood at the edge
of their lives, a mile above the river flowing, no, raging
        between red rock walls.

Ha, said the poet's son. *I remember*
my mother and I sat in the car
and watched my father pace back
and forth outside the ranger's station
at the canyon. Hell, we never
even got close to the actual

canyon. My father was all pissed off
because my mom hated the outdoors.
He gave us both the silent treatment
when we drove back to the motel.

Later on, my mother and I went out
for hamburgers while my father sat in the room
and wrote that goddamn poem.

Yes, yes, yes, let us now celebrate
fathers and sons, mothers and daughters
for we are all of those things.

Please, please, please, let us now celebrate
poets and liars, liars and poets
for we are both of those things.

Let us now celebrate the poet
who splashed his drink in the face
of the undergraduate woman
who would not *kneel and suck his cock*
during the English Department party.

That poet would never use
suck and cock in the same line
of a poem. Too percussive for him.
He employs long vowels
and soft consonants to seduce us. He fills
the rooms of his poem
with classical furniture. In his libido

There is no room for the post-modern.
His penis is a penis is a penis, the tool
of a working man, an artisan, sure
and simple. He compares the labia
with one flower or another, maybe all of them.

Let us now celebrate what may or may not be true.
Let us now celebrate the lies
that should be true because they tell us so much.
Let us now celebrate apocrypha.

Let us now celebrate the poet
who asked the woman for her name
as she stood in a long line
to receive one of his autographed books.

You better remember my name, she said.
You fucked me last night."

I want to find that woman. I want her to be
the pretty one walking down the street. I want her
to be Annabel Lee. I want her to be the lady in red.
I want her to be the blue eyes on Gatsby's wall.
I want her to be the poet with revenge on her mind.

Let us now celebrate the literary allusion.
Let us now celebrate the trope and the willful
enjambment. Let us now celebrate
the assonance and alliteration of all of it.
Let us now celebrate the sound of our own voices.

Let us now celebrate the long affairs between poets.
Let us now celebrate the one-night stands between poets.
Let us now celebrate the quick marriage and quicker divorce.
Let us now celebrate the fist and bruised face.
Let us now celebrate the knife.

Let us now celebrate the poet who shot at his wife
but missed once, twice, three times. Thank God
he was a better poet than marksman.
Thank God for his poems: bitter, rude, profane.
Thank God for his poems: racist, sexist, pornographic.
Thank God for his poems: lovely, lovely, lovely.
Thank God he wrote love poems to his son
even as he beat the boy bloody into corners.

Let us now celebrate the poet who wrote odes
to her husband on the skin of her lover's back.

Let us now celebrate the poet whose poems adorn
the walls of museums, the walls of museums
while her children are raised by somebody else's parents.

Yes, yes, yes, let us now celebrate the children
of poets. Let us now celebrate the husbands and wives
of poets. Let us now celebrate the mothers
and fathers of poets. Let us now celebrate the neighbors

of poets who are kept awake by the constant clatter
of keys and teeth. Let us now celebrate the lovers
of poets. Let us now celebrate the pets of poets: the kicked
pooch and the starving kitten, the venerated horse
and sacrificial cow, the kissing fish and fossilized hamster.

Let us now celebrate the poet
who put the shotgun to his head
and blew his genius brains
into a glass of orange juice.

Let us now celebrate the poet
who put her head into the oven.

Let us now celebrate the other poet
who put her head into the oven.

Let us now celebrate the man who married them both
and wrote the poems he orated when he buried them both.

Let us now celebrate the muse, his muse and her muse, your
        muse and my muse, their muse and our muse.

Yes, yes, yes, the poets prowl the aisles
of supermarkets and airplanes. They ride bicycles
through urban parks. They climb mountains
that have already been climbed. They pay for dinner.
They tell lies. They test drive the latest Ford
and the most recent Chevrolet. They teach
our children the difference between simile
and metaphor. They tell lies. They go to movies
and weep at happy endings. They tell lies.
They sing in the shower. Most sing poorly.
All of them tell lies. All of them tell lies.

Let us always celebrate the poets.

Please, please, please, the poets are scattered around the room
like stars. They blink and stutter. They are light
years away from us. They could die
today and news of their death, the shutting
off, would not reach us for decades.

The American Artificial Limb Company

My sister, my phantom limb, I reach for her
using her as the tool by which to remember her.

I wake at four in the morning with her fingers
on my throat. "Run now," she says. "On one leg
or three, it doesn't matter which." As the years pass

she becomes vestigial, an archaic organ
whose only purpose is to be removed. Today, I saw

a legless boy in a wheelchair, two women with hooks
for hands, and a man playing basketball on two prosthetic legs.
Grief attaches itself to my legs

with bolts and screws; grief
crushes my ribs beneath its weight; grief creates
new joints, new elbows and knees; grief removes
my hands and replaces them with more grief. Drunk

with grief and its whiskey, I once told
a pretty white woman she looked exactly
like my sister, but I lied. I also lied when I said
I only told one pretty white woman she looked
exactly like my sister. In truth, I have lost track
of the number of pretty white women who
looked exactly like my sister. I must have said that
to a dozen, to dozens. And, in truth yet again, I must
admit that none of the pretty white women
looked anything like my sister. I just wanted them

to rescue me. I was lonesome. On the highway, I was
the abandoned shoe that keens for its mate. When
I say she was my sister, I mean she was my sister.
You have to understand that white people invented

irony. I drive my car to the Veterans Hospital and watch
them lug pieces of men in and out, in and out, and in
and out. Remember, the photographs only reveal half

of her beauty, the other half being her dirty mouth
because she cursed as Whitman might have cursed
if Whitman had decided to curse the world instead
of praising it: Fuck the world, fuck the inadequate body

that housed my sister, fuck the arms and legs, fuck the fire
that took her away, fuck her for leaving, fuck the shovel
and glove, fuck the sheer competence of fork and knife
and spoon, fuck memory, fuck the clock, fuck oxygen, fuck
the amputees and their loneliness, fuck the inadequate
body that houses me, fuck beauty, fuck the shoe, fuck
the song, fuck irony, fuck this war and that war, fuck this
war and that war, fuck this and fuck that, fuck this, fuck
that, fuck, fuck, fuck, fuck, fuck, fuck, fuck, fuck, fuck.

"Sir," says the salesman, "Our artificial limbs come
in three different colors: white, black, and in-between."

One Stick Song

and so now, near the end of the game
when I only have one stick left to lose

and so now, near the end of the game
when I only have one stick left to lose

I will sing a one-stick song
I will sing a one-stick song

to bring back all the other sticks
to bring back all the other sticks

I will sing of my uncle
and the vein that burst in his head

o, bright explosion, crimson and magenta
o, kind uncle, brown skin and white T-shirt

o, crimson, magenta
o, brown, white

o, crimson
o, brown

o, uncle, kind uncle
I sing you back, I sing you back

and I will sing of my cousin
who jumped off the bridge

o, bright explosion, crimson and magenta
o, falling cousin, pink marrow and white water

o, crimson, magenta
o, pink, white

o, crimson
o, pink

o, cousin, falling cousin
I sing you back, I sing you back

and I will sing of my grandfather
killed by the sniper on Okinawa

o, bright explosion, crimson and magenta
o, soldier grandfather, green uniform and white sand

o, crimson, magenta
o, green, white

o, crimson
o, green

o, grandfather, soldier grandfather
I sing you back, I sing you back

and I will sing of the uncle
crushed beneath the fallen tree

o, bright explosion, crimson and magenta
o, small uncle, silver axe and white wood

o, crimson, magenta
o, silver, white

o, crimson
o, silver

o, uncle, small uncle
I sing you back, I sing you back

and I will sing of my grandmother
and her lover called tuberculosis

o, bright explosion, crimson and magenta
o, coughing grandmother, red blood and white handkerchief

o, crimson, magenta
o, red, white

o, crimson
o, red

o, grandmother, coughing grandmother
I sing you back, I sing you back

and I will sing of my aunt
who looked back and turned into a pillar of sugar

o, bright explosion, crimson and magenta
o, diabetic aunt, yellow skin and white tower

o, crimson, magenta
o, yellow, white

o, crimson
o, yellow

o, aunt, diabetic aunt
I sing you back, I sing you back

and I will sing of my cousin
who hitchhiked over the horizon

o, bright explosion, crimson and magenta
o, lost cousin, turquoise ring and white scar

o, crimson, magenta
o, turquoise, white

o, crimson
o, turquoise

o, cousin, lost cousin
I sing you back, I sing you back

and I will sing of my sister
asleep when her trailer burned

o, bright explosion, crimson and magenta
o, burned sister, scarlet skin and white ash

o, crimson, magenta
o, scarlet, white

o, crimson
o, scarlet

o, sister, burned sister
I sing you back, I sing you back

and I will sing of my uncle
and his lover called cirrhosis

o, bright explosion, crimson and magenta
o, swollen uncle, black liver and white hair

o, crimson, magenta
o, black, white

o, crimson
. o, black

o, uncle, swollen uncle
I sing you back, I sing you back

and I will sing of my grandmother
heavy with tumors

o, bright explosion, crimson and magenta
o, big grandmother, gold uranium and white X-ray

o, crimson, magenta
o, gold, white

o, crimson
o, gold

o, grandmother, big grandmother
I sing you back, I sing you back

and I will sing of my cousin
shot in the head by a forgetful man

o, bright explosion, crimson and magenta
o, drunk cousin, gray matter and white bone

o, crimson, magenta
o, gray, white

o, crimson
o, gray

o, cousin, drunk cousin
I sing you back, I sing you back

I sing you back, I sing all of you back
I sing you back, I sing all of you back

I sing you back from the parking lot of the convenience store
I sing you back from the sixth floor of the Catholic hospital
I sing you back from the seventh floor of the Veterans Hospital
back from the floor of your trailer house
from the cold fog of San Francisco
from 544 East Dave Court
I sing you back from the blood-stained wall
from the stand of pine
the Pacific Ocean
the Spokane River
I sing you back from Chimacum Creek.

I sing you back, I sing all of you back
I sing you back, I sing all of you back

and so now, near the end of the game
when I only have one stick left to win with

and so now, near the end of the game
when I only have one stick left to win with

I will sing a one-stick song
I will sing a one-stick song

to celebrate all of my sticks
returned to me

to celebrate all of my sticks
returned to me

returned to me
returned to me

returned to me
returned to me

Secondhand Grief

After his father dies
The son wears his clothes.

First, the black shoes
then the wool pants

and finally the blazer
with nostalgic lapels.

When he was a child
walking with his father

both of them wearing
identical suits and ties

the neighbors marveled
at how much they looked alike.

A thousand miles away
from his father's grave

He steps into his favorite overcoat
and then steps outside

to walk among fathers
and sons, strangers

strangers, strangers
strangers, strangers

strangers, strangers
strangers, all of them.

The Warriors

Opening Day

I hate baseball. I hate it because of its patriotic and inaccurate claim to be "America's game." Baseball may be the most popular sport in the United States, but the North American Canadians love hockey, and the Central and South Americans have turned soccer into a religion. I hate baseball because of its exaggerated reputation for magic and poetry. For every poetic and magical athlete like Ozzie Smith, a Langston Hughes-of-the-diamond, bebop, improvisational jazzman shortshop, there is a Charles Bukowski-on-deck, beer-swilling, big-bellied, tobacco-spitting baseball player like John Kruk. I hate baseball because John Kruk said, in defense of his Bukowski-esque physique, that he was a baseball player, not an athlete. I hate baseball because George Will, the right-wing conservative pundit, loves it so much. I hate baseball for the same reason George Will loves it: there are so many white men in the uniforms.

I hate baseball for many reasons. But I mostly hate it because on a hot summer day in 1979, in Wellpinit, Washington, on the Spokane Indian Reservation, I turned out for the Spokane Indian Little League baseball team called the Warriors, and while standing in the batting box for the very first time, facing the pitcher, Randy Peone, who was hurling fearsome fastballs and prodigal curveballs past me, I discovered that I could not see the ball as it left Randy's hand, and so naturally could not hit the ball, and though I still made the team because of my barely competent fielding skills, I knew I was destined for mediocrity as a baseball player.

Designated Hitter

Randy Peone, the blue-eyed Spokane Indian, was the star pitcher and shortstop. He was a short, stout, and handsome boy with a terrible temper. He came to Wellpinit in 1978, after having spent his earlier years at a school just off the reservation, and was immediately challenged to a fight by Stevie Flett, one of the school bullies. Fistfights were common among the Indian boys on my reservation. We were kids searching for some way to demonstrate our physical strength, courage, and leadership abilities. We desperately wanted to be traditional Indian warriors. Generations earlier, we might have hunted deer, battled against neighboring tribes and the United States Cavalry, sung traditional songs together, and war-danced in the same circle. However, in the absence of these traditions, we brutalized each other and established a hierarchy of contemporary warriors. When Randy showed up for his first day of school in Wellpinit, I was on the very bottom of that hierarchy and Stevie Flett was somewhere near the top. Stevie decided to test Randy.

Standing in a circle of Indian boys, Randy and Stevie traded generic insults, made promises to injure each other in specific ways, and challenged each other to throw the first punch. Then I watched Randy throw the punch that started at his toes, worked its way up his leg, through his hip and ribcage, down his muscular arm, and into the scarred fist that broke Stevie Flett's nose. The fight was over that quickly, and just as quickly, Randy had radically changed our established hierarchy. With one punch, with Stevie Flett's broken nose, Randy had established himself as our chief. He could be a powerful ally or dangerous enemy. As the lowest and weakest of Indian braves, I was required to worship Randy, and I did, in fact, worship him. Despite and because of that worship, Randy and I became friends. I admired his boastful confidence and athletic ability. I envied the romantic attention he received from Indian and white girls. I don't know what he saw in me. I was a quiet, painfully serious, and scholarly boy who cried too easily. I couldn't play baseball and though I was somehow a good basketball player, despite my obvious lack of athletic ability in any other sport, I would never be as good as Randy. We were complete opposites who became best friends. I told him my deepest secrets. I wept over my unrequited love of Indian girls like Dawn Flett, Lu Lu Samuels, Jana Wynne, and Lori Schatzer. I confessed my secret desire to leave the reservation for college and never come back. Randy listened to me. He kept my secrets safe. However, despite our friendship, he was still the chief and I was just a brave.

During a roadtrip that Little League summer, Randy tried to pants me, meaning that he wanted to strip me to my underwear in front of all the Indian girls who also played on our team. He wanted to prove his power over me. He wanted to show the others that his friendship with me had not weakened him. Feeling angry and betrayed, I punched Randy in the eye. In retaliation, he punched me and broke my nose. Any respect I momentarily gained by punching Randy was quickly lost as I cupped my bleeding nose and bawled like a baby. Randy and I didn't speak for a few days afterwards and made a theatrical display of avoiding each other. But, slowly and carefully, we became friends again, as boys do, by choosing the same food in restaurants, by laughing at the same dirty jokes, by playing on the same baseball team. During a critical game one week after he broke my nose, Randy drove in the go-ahead run in the top of the last inning, and then, in the bottom of the inning, I ran in crazy and confused circles in right field and somehow caught the towering fly ball that ended the game. Randy and I danced circles around each other as we celebrated our victory.

A Lexical Interlude

A reservation Little League baseball team called the Warriors? Indians recognize irony when we see it. During that summer, irony played third base.

In the Batter's Box

I literally could not hit the ball. I swung and whiffed, swung and whiffed, swung and whiffed. My teammates would cheer on those rare occasions when I managed to hit even a foul ball. I must have struck out in my first fifty or sixty plate appearances that summer, though I never once grounded into a doubleplay because I never once hit a grounder while anybody was on base. I was a complete loser at the plate. I only played because I was a decent right fielder, if there is such a thing in Little League baseball, and because Randy Peone's father, Cub, was the coach.

"Keep your eye on the ball!" Cub would shout to me as I stood in the warmup circle and took a few practice swings. "Keep the bat level! Keep your back foot planted! Step forward into the pitch! Make the pitcher throw strikes! Take one for the team! Concentrate! Bat speed, bat speed, bat speed!"

I was afraid of batting. I wasn't exactly afraid of the ball, or being hit by the ball, though I was beaned twice that summer and cried both times. I was afraid of failing, of the very concept of failure. I was a star student and a good basketball player who, during a game, could physically embarrass all of the Indian boys who beat me up before and after the game. In the classroom, while taking a test or raising my hand to answer a question, I believed I was a better person than at any other time during my life. My grades became the most accurate measure of my self-esteem. I would feel great for a few hours after I aced a test, but I'd be depressed for days if I happened to answer even one question incorrectly. I read books with a ferocity that turned the flipping of pages into a violent act. As I raced through a mathematics test, filling in the right answers almost reflexively, I felt like I could conquer the world. In the classroom, I was chief. However, in the batter's box, I was nobody, nothing, the bottom of the barrel, the strikeout king, Mr. oh-for, the automatic out. In the batter's box, I was ugly, stupid, and insignificant. I was a complete failure.

During that Little League summer, I trembled with fear each time I walked to the plate, stepped into the batter's box, and stared at the opposing pitcher. My batting ritual was always the same. I would tap the base with my bat, plant my right foot in the dirt, grit my teeth, inhale, exhale, and then swing at three straight pitches, no matter where they were thrown, and miss all of them. I swung at wild pitches that flew five feet over the catcher's head and wedged themselves in the chainlink fence behind home plate. Dejected, I would walk back to the dugout, throw my batting helmet to the ground, and flop on the bench. Nobody would say a word to me.

A Philosophical Interlude

A few years ago, I drove up to Chewelah, Washington, to watch my little brother James play T-ball, a slightly ridiculous and altogether democratic version of baseball where there are no pitched balls. Instead, the batter takes swings at a ball carefully balanced on a tee that is in turn carefully balanced on home plate. The little six- and seven-year olds take mighty swings at the ball and send it dribbling into play where, seemingly, dozens of infielders chase it around the diamond. There is much laughter and confusion as players abandon their positions in pursuit of the ball. Most singles happen because the first baseman has abandoned his position and is chasing a ball down the third base line. Most doubles happen because an excited kid will field a ball and throw it toward an empty first base, allowing the runner to advance as the ball skips into the thick grass of foul territory. Most triples occur when the defensive team cannot then find that ball. Strictly speaking, there are an awesome number of infield homeruns. However, there are very few balls hit into the outfield. In fact, during my little brother's T-ball career, I never saw one ball hit into the outfield.

On that particular day in Chewelah, James was the right fielder. In the third inning, James tore off his glove, threw it the ground, and sat down in the damp grass. Disgusted and angry, he refused to stand up and take his position, no matter how loud we yelled at him. The coach, having no other option, quickly sent in a substitute.

"James," I said as we drove home after the game. "You shouldn't have done that. You've got to be ready for anything."

"Nobody hits balls out there," he said and began to cry. He was so young and understood so much. "It's a waste."

"But you never know," I said. "It could happen."

"It never happens," he said. "Nothing ever happens in right field."

A League of Their Own

Five or six or seven Spokane Indian girls played on the Warriors that Little League summer. I believe Michelle Andrews, Melissa Williams, Kim Kuhns, Karen Williams, Sabrina Boyd, and Yolanda Wynne played, though I cannot be sure, and there were others I certainly cannot remember now. I cannot remember all of the boys who played either (Todd Holt was probably on the team, but I cannot recall one specific memory of him from that summer), but I feel worse about forgetting the girls' names. In this, I feel sexist and shallow.

What do I remember about those Little League Indian girls? I was not in love with any of them, although I did "go" with

Michelle Andrews for about fifteen minutes in fifth grade and with Karen Williams for a day or so that same year. During Little League, I resented those girls because they were all just as horrible at baseball as I was. We were all interchangeable as players, and that was simply unacceptable to a twelve-year-old Indian boy who was trying to be a reservation warrior. Those girls often took my place in the batting order and at my position in right field. I burned with shame as I watched them strike out on three straight pitches, just as I would have, and let fly balls drop to the outfield grass, just as I would have. None of those girls were very athletic. I don't think any of them played sports later in high school, though Michelle Andrews eventually left the reservation and became a cheerleader at a neighboring school. I don't know where she is now. Melissa Williams was a smart girl who was supposed to have gone to college, though she still had not left the reservation when I talked to her last. Yolanda still lives on the reservation and usually plays right field on a co-ed softball team. I don't know anything about Kim Kuhns and Sabrina Boyd. I know Karen Williams still lives in Wellpinit and has a few children, though I know neither their names nor their ages, neither their genders nor their faces. I don't remember much about those Little League Indian girls and I don't know much about the Indian women they have become. Though I lived in Wellpinit until I was eighteen, I attended high school in an-all white farm town just off the reservation. After high school, I went to college and, except for a few months after I graduated, have never again lived on the reservation. I am now as distant from those Spokane Indian girls as some other planet is from earth. Yet, like a spy satellite, I orbit silently around those girls and write my poems and stories in a vain attempt to map our differences, to control the weather, to reveal our secrets.

My secret? I would have had sex, or at least performed all of those physical acts that I imagined to be sex, with any of those Little League Indian girls if they had let me. I was a twelve-year old boy just beginning to see the bloom in women, the beauty of their forms. Even as I resented those Indian girls for taking my spot in the field, I sat on the bench and studied their bodies with adolescent lust. I didn't love them, but I wanted to touch their small breasts, flat asses, brown thighs, and long, black hair. I didn't think any of those girls were as beautiful as white girls, though a couple were definitely pretty, but I still loved to sit beside any one of them and breath in her intoxicating scent of perfume and sweat. I suppose I'm not revealing much of a secret here. I'm sure almost every boy trembles excitedly in the presence of girls. I know almost every man trembles excitedly in the presence of women. But my lust, my individual, aboriginal, and imaginative lust felt like a dangerous bomb during that Little League summer. I didn't know how to defuse it. Hell, I didn't want to defuse it. I fell in love with my lust.

My other secret? I lusted after white girls and women more than I lusted after Indian girls and women. Television taught me to do this. Television taught me that the bodies of white women were more beautiful than the bodies of brown women. Television taught me that white skin was inherently good and pure, and that brown skin was inherently evil and dirty. On television, white men were heroes and Indian men were savages. On television, Indian women were primitive and ugly, and white women were primitive and gorgeous. I learned to hate my brown skin and came to believe that if I could touch the bare skin of a white woman I could somehow change myself. I dreamed about touching the pale skin of television beauties like Farrah Fawcett, Kate Jackson, and Jacklyn Smith as Charlie's Angels, like Linda Carter as Wonder Woman, like Lindsay Wagner as the Bionic Woman. I can remember, with a startling and vivid clarity, the day I picked up a movie magazine and saw a photograph of Lindsay Wagner with her brown-skinned Indian husband. I brought that magazine home and fantasized over that photograph for months. I closed my eyes and thought of white women, of white skin, of pale thighs and bellies, of creamy breasts and necks, of blonde pubic hair and ivory feet. During that Little League summer, during all of my reservation summers, I desperately dreamed about leaving Wellpinit, about leaving all of those Indian women behind me. I wanted to go to college and never come back. I wanted to have sex with white women simply because they were white women. I studied that photograph of Lindsay Wagner and her Indian husband. He was not all that handsome. He had a fat face, pock-marked skin, and shaggy hair. I wondered why he got to have sex with the Bionic Woman. I decided he must be very smart, and I came to believe that my chances of sleeping with a beautiful white woman increased exponentially with each book I read. And believe me, I read a lot of books. I read novels, autobiographies, and historical non-fiction. I read poetry, chemistry textbooks, and Westerns. I read celebrity profiles, science fiction, and auto repair manuals. Once again, I suppose I'm not revealing much of a secret here. After all, I have since had sex with and fallen in love with white women. I loved a white woman who once told me she hated Indians. I loved a white woman whose parents were afraid she and I would produce "charcoal babies." Obviously, my lust for white women was also a dangerous bomb that constantly threatened to destroy any number of lives. No, I didn't know how to defuse that bomb. But, as I grew a little older, I realized that I wanted to defuse that bomb. I was no longer in love with my lust for white women.

I have since met, fallen in love with, and married a Hidatsa/Ho Chunk/Potawatomi Indian woman who doesn't play baseball. She has beautiful, clear, brown skin and long, raven-black hair. She has a master of arts degree in theology and can make me laugh until I cry. Has my love (and undeniable lust) for my wife "cured" me of my lust (and undeniable love) for white women? No, of course not. I enjoyed watching the blonde-haired and pale-skinned Helen Hunt, wearing a tight white T-shirt, as she smartly dodged tornadoes in the movie Twister.

I have a crush on Tori Amos, the ethereal, piano-playing, and very eccentric singer-songwriter. I lost my breath when I first saw Amy Ray, one half of the folk duo Indigo Girls, as she switched gender roles and played the big man himself in a production of Jesus Christ Superstar. I have had a lifelong crush on Jane Pauley. So what's the difference between my lust and love for white women now and the lust and love I felt for white women when I was a teenager? I know now that a white woman could never love me in the way an Indian woman can. An Indian woman will love me, in good and bad ways, as an Indian woman. That cannot be replicated, imitated, replaced, or mimicked. I know now that white skin is not magical. The white women I touched were ordinary people who lived ordinary lives. I remember them with fondness, the slight remains of love, and a definite measure of regret. I know now there is something redemptive in loving an Indian woman. I feel as if I'm somehow forgiven for my years of ignoring Indian women. I know that Indian women are proud of me for choosing to love an Indian woman, especially since many highly successful Indian men choose white women.

At a recent Native American awards banquet, speaker after speaker extolled the virtues of all the highly successful Indian men in the audience. They were brave, intelligent, loving, and respectful leaders. They were warriors. Everybody clapped in agreement. The Indian men clapped for themselves. Then, late in the evening, an elder Indian woman took the podium.

"I hear all this talk about Indian men here," she said. "How they are brave and intelligent, how they are the new warriors. But I look around at all of you Indian men and see the white women seated beside you. And I wonder what I should tell my granddaughter. What does it say to my granddaughter that all of you brave and intelligent warriors are with white women? What does it say to my granddaughter that the most successful Indian men choose to spend their lives with white women? What should I tell my granddaughter about this?"

I was not there when that elder Indian woman spoke this truth. I heard this story from an Indian man who was there. He laughed at the memory. I laughed with him, though I wanted to cry as well. What indeed will that elder tell her granddaughter? What should I say here to Melissa Williams, Michelle Andrews, Kim Kuhns, Karen Williams, Sabrina Boyd, and Yolanda Wynne? I can see them in their Little League uniforms, white T-shirts with blue sleeves. with their last names and numbers stenciled on the back, and THE WARRIORS stenciled on the front. What could I say to them? I didn't love them when they were girls. I barely know them now as adults. Will I visit their homes, share bread at their tables, and tell them I should have loved them, and would have loved them, if I'd given myself the chance? No, of course not. They are gone from my life. They live and love in worlds I have never visited. In my world, those Little League Indian girls have become ghosts who haunt me at specific moments, in specific places. If I stood on the baseball diamond in Wellpinit, I would hear their voices and laughter. I could breathe in their sweet scent. I could apologize.

Spokane Indian women, I'm sorry. I grew up distant and always afraid.

A Nostalgic Interlude

My father always used to tell me that he was so poor he had to use a left-handed catcher's mitt when he played second base for his Little League team in Coeur d'Alene, Idaho.

I never believed him until I came across an old black-and-white photograph of my father, twelve years old and impossibly beautiful, with a left-handed catcher's mitt tied loosely to his belt.

Stratomatic Indians

Steve LeBret, my next door neighbor and brother-by-proclamation, formed the very first Spokane Indian Reservation Stratomatic Baseball league that Little League summer. Stratomatic Baseball is a complicated board game, complete with dice, charts, and statistical representations of each and every Major League player, that faithfully recreates entire games and seasons. That summer, Steve, my oldest brother Arnold, Rich Flett, and I drafted all-star teams and played dozens of games against each other. As best as I can remember, this was my first roster:

STARTERS:
1B: Eddie Murray, Baltimore Orioles
2B: Joe Morgan, Houston Astros
3B: Mike Schmidt, Philadelphia Phillies
SS: Dave Concepcion, Cincinnati Reds
OF: David Kingman, Chicago Cubs
OF: Gorman Thomas, Milwaukee Brewers
OF: Dave Parker, Pittsburgh Pirates
C: Johnny Bench, Cincinnati Reds

RESERVES:
Willie Stargell, Pittsburgh Pirates
Pete Rose, Cincinnati Reds
Steve Garvey, Los Angeles Dodgers
Greg Luzinski, Philadelphia Phillies
Oscar Moreno, New York Yankees
Robin Yount, Milwaukee Brewers
Steve Yeager, Los Angeles Dodgers

PITCHERS:
Jim Palmer, Baltimore Orioles
Kent Tekulve, Pittsburgh Pirates
Tom Seaver, New York Mets
Steve Carlton, Philadelphia Phillies
Ron Guidry, New York Yankees
Goose Gossage, Oakland Athletics
Mike Marshall, Minnesota Twins
Steve Stone, Baltimore Orioles

Of course, I could be completely wrong about this roster. I recall now that Eddie Murray was one of Steve LeBret's favorite players. It seems inconceivable that Steve, who often rigged the games in his favor, would let me have one of his favorite players. I look at the names "Oscar Moreno" and "Steve Yeager," and I seriously have to wonder if I invented those players. Have I created two people who never existed? I believe that Steve Yeager wore glasses and was a catcher. I have no visual image of Oscar Moreno, though I think he was an outfielder. Am I lying to myself? Am I telling a lie which, because of its placement here, becomes a kind of story?

In later years, our Stratomatic Baseball League would grow to include players of every generation. I can remember the names of some of my favorite players, though I cannot tell you if they were a part of my roster:

C: Roy Campanella, Dodgers
1B: Lou Gehrig, Yankees
2B: Nap Lajoie, team unknown
3B: Brooks Robinson, Orioles
SS: Pee Wee Reese, Dodgers
OF: Tris Speaker, team unknown
OF: Hack Wilson, team unknown
OF: Duke Snider, Dodgers
P: Chief Bender, Indians
P: Juan Marichal, Orioles
P: Early Wynn, team unknown
P: Sandy Koufax, Dodgers
P: Bob Gibson, team unknown

I wonder about these baseball players. They existed for me as names on a Stratomatic playing card. For me, they were all bundles of statistics. If I managed them correctly and rolled a pair of lucky dice, I could win games. I could pitch the ball with the blinding speed of Nolan Ryan. I could hit the ball with the deadly efficiency of Rod Carew. I could play outfield with the grace of Willie Mays. Or I could manage the players poorly by forgetting to sacrifice bunt, by ignoring the crucial difference between left- and right-handed pitchers, or by allowing my favorite players to play despite any errors they continued to make.

During that summer, between Stratomatic Baseball games, my brother Arnold made the error of driving while intoxicated and nearly killed himself in a car wreck on the west end of the reservation. Late on a weekend night, he drove his pickup through a guardrail and rolled down a steep hill. He was thrown out of the pickup and it somehow leapfrogged over him. He had a concussion, facial lacerations, and a broken right collarbone. I didn't want to visit him in the hospital. I was afraid of hospitals. But more than that, I was afraid of seeing my powerful brother lying in a hospital bed. I didn't want to see him looking so fragile and weak in his hospital gown.

"I don't want to go," I said to my mother.

"But it's your brother," she said.

"I don't like hospitals."

She understood. She didn't care much for hospitals either. But she forced me to go anyway and when I finally saw my brother, he looked far worse than I had even imagined. He was pale and looked as if he'd lost twenty pounds overnight. Due to the painkillers, he slurred through a disjointed monologue and his eyes were glazed over. I wanted to cry.

When he came home a few days after the accident, he wanted to play me a game of Stratomatic Baseball. With his arm in a sling, he set out his lineup, rolled the dice, and proceeded to kick my ass. He was ahead by an ungodly amount of runs by the third inning. I watched him carefully. He smiled. He taunted me. My brother is one of the most competitive people I have ever known. His favorite player was Jose Cruz, outfielder for the Houston Astros. Jose hit four or five home runs that day. Jose was beautiful. My brother was beautiful. I wanted them both to live forever. But more than that, I wanted to beat my brother. I wanted to win.

"You stink," I said to my brother. And he did stink. His sling was damp with summer sweat. His breath smelled of some medicine or another.

"What?" he asked.

"You smell bad."

I knew I had hurt his feelings. But he was my older brother and could not show it.

"You should take a shower," I said.

He ignored me, rolled the dice, and one of his players drove in a run. He rolled the dice again and another one of his players hit a home run. Or a triple, or a double, or single. It doesn't matter. My brother was winning the game. I loved him. I hated him. He had almost died. He was alive.

Extra Innings

In my dreams, I step up to the plate and the bases are loaded with beautiful Indian women. Randy Peone is pitching. My older brother Arnold is catching. Nobody is playing the field. Arnold calls for the fast ball. Randy throws the heat. For the first time in my life, I can see the ball as it leaves his fingers, as it slowly drifts toward me, as I realize I'll be able to hit the ball farther than I have ever hit it, as I choke up on the bat, as I dig in my right heel, as I lift my left foot and step forward toward the pitch. I swing and swing and swing. I hate baseball.

Migration, 1902

The salmon swim
so thick in this river

that Grandmother walks
across the water

on the bridge
of their spines.

A Poem Written in Replication of My Father's Unfinished Novel Which He Would Read to His Children Whenever He Was Drunk

Indian summer. Leaves fallen
from government trees. They remind me of sex.

My mother and father dead.
My father fell

at Okinawa, shot by a Japanese sniper.
I do not hate the Japanese. My lover is

Japanese. She reminds me of sex.
Pregnant, my mother coughed

blood into paper tissue.
She died two weeks after I was born.

Now my Japanese lover is pregnant. She whispers
stories to her stomach about a small island

in the Pacific where her father killed
an American soldier during the war.

My lover and I wonder aloud
if her father killed my father.

We shiver in the heat of it.
It reminds us of sex.

After my parents died, I lived
with my aunt, who had enough money

to send me to Catholic school. I was
the only Indian who went to Catholic school

on purpose. I learned to play piano.
I jitterbugged with Catholic girls

and their pale thighs.
They smelled like sex.

I fell in love with all of them.
I learned chord after chord. Sex.

Often, these days, I stand at the window
of my reservation home

while my Japanese lover sleeps alone
in the scattered bed. She is pregnant.

Her father and mother live
with the dead in Hiroshima.

My father and mother are also dead.
Piano. Chord after chord. Island.

That window. This window.
One Indian boy runs

blindly through the trees.
A shadow falls

over everything.
Sex. Leaf, Faith. Glass.

If I stand at this window long enough
I will see the long thread of history

float randomly through the breeze.
This is all I know about peace.

Memorial Day, 1972

I was too young to clean graves
so I waded into the uranium river
carrying the cat who later gave birth
to six headless kittens.

O, Lord, remember, O, do remember me.

The Hunger Psalm, 1973

After the Indian money was gone
and we had eaten the last of the food
our mother and father drove into the city
and pawned their wedding rings.

Praise, praise
praise the left hand.

The Mice War

We dumped six garbage cans and watched dozens of mice
race for their lives across the gray sand of the reservation
landfill. With shovel and broom stick, my cousin and I

chased them down. I beheaded twenty-seven before I
simply beat one mouse into a red puddle. The reservation
had taught me to hate, so it was easy to hate the mice.

I swung the shovel until my hands blistered. I killed mice
because they were mice. I swung the shovel until I
could barely raise my arms. I hated the reservation

because it was the reservation. It was my reservation.
I swung that shovel until the surviving mice
ran into the thick grass on the perimeter of the fill. I

chased them down. I beat the grass because it was grass. I
hated the grass because the reservation
had taught me to hate grass. I chased that last mouse

into the last corner. There, in that place, I
stepped on that mouse because it was a part of all mice.
I broke its spine because my reservation

believed in broken spines, because my reservation
believed in blood, because my reservation believed in mice
and the broken spines and the blood of mice. Because I

believed in the blood of mice, I kneeled to pray when I
discovered blood on my shoes. O, Lord, the blood of mice.
O, Lord, the broken back of my reservation

trembles and stirs. The fault line that bisects my reservation
shifts me from one sin to another, from the blood of one mouse
to another, from this prayer to that prayer. O, Lord, I

tossed the bloody shoes into the burning barrel. O, Lord, I
dropped the dead mice into the fire and the reservation
burned. O, Lord, this is how I remember my war with the mice

who, in the beginning and in the end, only wanted to be mice,
while we were two Indian boys, my cousin and I
who, in our beginning, in our end, wanted to flee the reservation.

Soon to be a National Geographic Special

All of the Indian boys in the world
gathered into one red Toyota Celica
or perhaps it was just Steve, Tom, and me
though, truthfully speaking, it wasn't Tom

at all. In fact, it was his brother Dan, but I want
to place Tom in the Celica with Steve
and me because Tom killed himself
a few years back, and I miss him.

I want to remember him
in some poem, in this particular poem
because I am a poet now, though
I wasn't a poet back then. Of course

Tom wasn't a poet and he wasn't
an Indian either, which means his brother
wasn't Indian, and Steve was only
a little bit Indian himself, but he grew up

on the reservation, and therefore
was a full Indian pretty much
by osmosis. So, now, to reiterate, the Toyota
was filled with all of the Indian boys

in the world (meaning there was one
white boy who was only there
metaphorically, one mostly-white boy
made Indian by association, and one

true and actual Indian boy) as the auto sped
through the reservation night, as
it insulted the cold air with the heat
of its arrival and passage, as we Indian boys

laughed at the impossibility
of the Northern Lights, as the Great Barn Owl
swooped down over the road, its epic wings
stretching from ditch to ditch, its epic wings

striking flames as it roared directly
toward all of the Indian boys
in the world, as Steve slammed
on the brakes, or more likely, it was Tom

who slammed on the brakes (meaning
that his brother Dan slammed
on the brakes) as that Great Barn Owl flew
just a few feet above the pavement

as it grew so large and impossible
in the headlights, as all of the Indian boys
in the world, in the Toyota Celica, decided
they were going to die, die, die

as that Great Barn Owl suddenly lifted
into the air, just barely avoiding
a terrible head-on collision, as the three of us
ducked our heads in reflex, as we turned

to look behind us, turned to look
at our past, at our future, as we turned to see
that Great Barn Owl disappear
somewhere behind the poker-faced moon.

Water

1

I know a woman
who swims naked in the ocean
no matter the season.

I don't have a reason
for telling you this

(I never witnessed
her early morning
dips into the salt)

other than to let you know
that I once found the thought
of her nudity erotic

but now can only imagine
the incredible cold, how
I would want to cover her body
with my coat and tell her
how crazy she is
for having so much faith

in two parts hydrogen, one part oxygen.

2

While reading a mystery novel (I
don't remember the title), I dropped

a cup of hot tea into my lap.
Third degree burns

on my thighs, penis, and scrotum.
I still carry the scars and once told

a white woman the burns were the result
of a highly sacred Indian ceremony

3

I knew a man
who drowned

in three inches of water
collected in a tire track.

I wish I could name him here
but tribal laws forbid me

to name the dead.
These laws are aboriginal

and more important
than any poem.

But I want to give him
a name

that means what I say
so I name him

Hamlet, King Lear
Othello, Noah, Adam.

4

Then Boo tells me, "Whenever I feel depressed or lonely
I drink a glass of water and immediately feel better."

5

In the unlikely event of a water landing
you can use your seat cushion as a flotation device.

I worry about this.

I wonder if the puny seat cushion can support
my weight. I am a large man. In the unlikely event
of a water landing, you can use your seat cushion
as a flotation device. Of course, the plane doesn't crash.
We land safely. We always land safely. And Ha! Ha!
The flight attendant tells the disembarking passengers
to drive safely away from the airport, because driving is
so much more dangerous, statistically speaking, than flying.

I'd like to slap her across the mouth, statistically speaking.

In the unlikely event of a water landing, you can use
your seat cushion as a flotation device. I am suddenly afraid
of gravity, so I take my seat cushion off the plane. I steal
the damn thing and run through the airport, chased
by an ever increasing number of security people, both
men and women, so I'm pleased this airport has progressed
beyond an antiquated notion of gender roles. But wait

I have no time to be liberal. I have to run fast
so I do run fast, with that seat cushion pressed tightly
against my chest. I cannot run fast enough
in such an awkward position, as I am a large man.
I cannot easily hide. I cannot blend into the crowd.
I cannot duck behind the counter of Burger King
and ask for your order, your order, your order.

Yes, in the event of water landing, you can use your seat cushion
as a flotation device, and here I am, running, and praying
as I run, every step shouting LORD, LORD, LORD
every other step whispering amen, amen, amen.

6

At the restaurant, a good one, I ask the waiter to leave
the pitcher of water because I drink lots of water.

"I can't do that," he says.

"Why not?" I ask.

"Because we never leave the pitcher," he says.

"Not once?" I ask.

"Never," he says, "have we ever left a whole pitcher
of water, not once in the entire history of this restaurant.
It is impossible for us to do so. It is inconceivable for us
to even consider doing such a thing. Who knows
what would happen if we set such a precedent?"

7

When I was seven, I took swim lessons
at the YMCA from three beautiful teenagers

who all seemed like women to me.
They hugged me when they saw me

waiting in line to see *Jaws* at the Fox Theater
in downtown Spokane. Where are they now?

Somewhere, those girls are being women.

Do they remember teaching me
how to swim? Do they recognize my face

when they pick up the local newspaper
or see my photograph on the back of this book?

O, strange, strange ego.

Here and now, I've decided I want them
to love me from afar. I want them to regret

their entire lives because they were once
sixteen-year-old swimmers who never stopped

to passionately kiss the seven-year-old me
as I floated from the deep end of the pool

back to the shallow.

8

My brother, the big one, says, "It ain't truly water
unless it's got three scoops of Kool-aid in it."

9

My wife, the Indian, grew up in Southern California
with a swimming pool in the backyard. Wow!

Her father, the trickster, called relatives back home
in North Dakota, called them in late December
when trees were exploding in the high plains cold.
He called them and said, "Hey, it's December

here in California, but the kids are still swimming
in the pool. Can you hear them splashing the water?"

Her father held that phone high into the air, toward
the empty pool. It was empty because it was too cold
to swim in December, even in Southern California
but the North Dakota Indians didn't know any better
so they were jealous and happy at the same time.

My wife, just a child then of five or ten or eighteen years
heard the slurred laughter of her father, the drunk.
He would shout into the phone. "Hey, it's December

here in sunny California, but the boys and girls are still
swimming in our pool. Can you hear them? Can you?"

My wife, just a child, heard her father on the telephone
and he would laugh and hang up and might be charming
or maybe he would be the cruel bastard, but there was no way
of knowing until he got off the phone, so she'd sit in her room

with a glass of water on the windowsill, and she'd be praying
to that glass of water, she'd be praying
to that telephone, she'd be praying to that swimming pool,
 she'd be praying to her father, she'd be praying

like everything was two parts broken heart and one part hope.

Sex in Motel Rooms

1

Because I need music
I press my ear to the wall

and listen to the lovers
in the next room

as they undress each other
as they undress each other.

The glorious
tintinnabulation

of one shirt, two shirts
clanging to the floor.

2

After she came
she rolled away

and fell off the edge
of the twin bed.

3

As I drive home
to the reservation

I pass by the motel
where a white girl I loved

during high school
lost her virginity
to a white boy
after the goddamn prom.

4

On the first night of our honeymoon
we lie in bed, too exhausted for sex

or conversation. Instead, we listen
to the surf, wave after wave after wave.

5

On the couch, X wants Y
to take off her pants

but she refuses
because her best friend, Z

is naked in bed
on the other side

of the room
with X's best friend, A

who is desperately
in love with Y.

6

O, the lonely country!
O, the lonely city!
O, the lonely motel!
O, the lonely bed!
O, the lonely man!

7

There are two beds in the room. Of course
we make love in one, fall asleep in the other.

8

Listen, she says, I always wanted
to watch a pornographic movie

in a hotel room, so my boyfriend
and I ordered one, pay-per-view

but it wasn't real porn. I mean,
they didn't show any penetration.

It was just a bunch of shots
of sweaty bellies and profiles,

really tame, generic stuff,
and it barely aroused us

so we just sort of kissed
and fondled each other

then fell asleep, still
wearing most of our clothes.

9

In the darkness, her dark body grows darker
until I am making love to her and her shadow.

10

In Santa Monica, over
the course of three nights

the woman in the next room
sleeps with three different men.

I watch them all arrive
through the security peephole

in my door. One of the men
is beautiful, one is ugly

and the third is a waiter
from the restaurant downstairs.

11

Scientists recently examined a hotel room comforter
and discovered 412 different samples of sperm.

12

Okay, he says, I'm not one of those guys
who sleeps with anything that moves

but the threat of AIDS prevented me
from even thinking

about becoming one of those guys.
AIDS is a shitty deal for everybody

but it's a really shitty deal for sex in general.
After all, our parents got to fuck

and fuck and fuck and fuck
without the fear of death.

I mean, I think all the liberalism
and progressive social change

during the Sixties happened
because everybody was fucking

like crazy. And I think we elected
and re-elected that right-wing Reagan asshole

because nobody was fucking.
That's right. Sex and politics

are linked. Tight as tight.
If it was up to me, I'd set up this motel

where sex was happening
in every room. Sex and food.

I mean, the mini-bars would be filled
with cheese and crackers and fruit.

Room service would be complimentary.
Good coffee machines.

Sex and jobs, too.
I mean, in order to participate

you'd have to work at the motel.
Janitor, maid, waiter, something.

Sex and love, of course.
I mean, if you wanted to, you could

just have sex with one person.
That would be permitted

maybe even encouraged.
Everybody would have enough sex

everybody would have enough food
and everybody would have a job.

13

Home with her
we get ready for bed

brush our teeth, wash our faces
all of those small ceremonies

and then we're beneath
the down comforter

on a cold Seattle night
and I'm almost asleep

when she moves close
kisses my ear and asks me

to pretend we're in the last
vacant motel room in the world.

The Anatomy of Mushrooms

Now, after all of these years, I remember the woman, whom
    I loved,
who casually mentioned that mushrooms reminded her of
    penises
though I cannot recall for sure if the comparison fascinated or
    repelled her.
Soon after that conversation, she left me for another woman

and though I too have since fallen in love with and married
another woman, I often pause in the middle of lovemaking
to think about the fog-soaked forest into which we all travel
to think about the damp, dank earth into which we all plunge
    our hands

to search for water and spore and root and loam
to search for water and room and roof and home.

Why Indian Men Fall in Love with White Women

"This is how it is," says the white woman in the donut shop
    (it wasn't
a donut shop but something else entirely) and then she laughs
a melodious, joyous noise, and she smacks a hand, her left one
I believe, to her forehead in mock-Lucy exasperation, and then
    says
again, "This is how it is," but then adds as an afterthought, or

considering the use of the pun, perhaps had planned on saying it
all along, saying "This is my job," except she doesn't say job, as
in work, she says Job, with a long vowel, as in the guy from the
    Bible.
Of course, this makes me love her, because if she said it
as an afterthought, then she is bright, but if she had always
    planned

to say it, to say Job, like the Job in the Bible, who had the worst
    job
in human history, then she is disciplined. She says "This is my
    Job,"
as an afterthought, or as part of her daily script, I don't care which.
She says Job with the job, the job belonging to Job, Job possessed
by his job, the Job, the job, the Job, the job. Is the white woman

in the donut shop really that clever, and let's admit it, the pun
is not truly that clever, but clever enough , perhaps too clever
for a woman working in a donut shop (but it wasn't really
a donut shop), but I don't really care to guess at the exact level
of her education, because she laughs so joyously, because her eyes

are blue and alive with happiness and intelligence, so I decide
right there in the donut shop, that she is indeed too clever to be
working in a donut shop, that she is, in fact, a scholar who turned
her back on her academic pursuits, that she was a theologian
a blessed and gifted woman who wanted to be a priest, a Jesuit

an Ignatian, of all things, but was turned back by the Catholic
     Church
and its antiquated notions of gender. She is romantic and novel
and more than a little sad, but she disguises her sadness so well
behind her blue eyes, though I am sensitive enough to see enough
of her sadness to guess at the whole of her sadness, even as she
     laughs

even as she takes my sympathetic order for a dozen donuts, as
     she gathers
the donuts into the appropriate container, as she hands it to me, as
our hands touch, as the tips of her fingers brush against the tips
of my fingers, as we briefly share a moment, and by "moment," I
     mean
a segment of immeasurable time, and in that moment, I feel
     forgiven

or perhaps I am merely aroused, sexually and/or spiritually, but
in either case, I take a donut (maple?) from my appropriate
     container
and offer it to her, and she takes it with delight (she still loves
donuts, despite the Job-ness of her job), and she bites into it
and chews it without suggestion. She chews simply

with and without grace. She chews like a monk. She is that flour;
she is that egg; she is that sugar; she is that water. She is that
     flour;
she is that egg; she is that sugar; she is that water; She is the
     whole
of the donut; she is the hole of the donuts. She is the blue tear
balanced on the lower lid of her left eye. She is Job, my dear Job.

Powwow Love Songs

1

"Mating birds and mating Indians are the same," says a white
  friend as we watch the handsome fancydancers
in their red, yellow, orange, and blue feathers. "It's the men
  who wear the brightest colors."

2

When I want an Indian woman to notice me, I wear a red shirt
  that smells like a powwow:
campfire smoke, fry bread smoke, burning tobacco smoke,
  burning sage smoke, burning sweetgrass smoke
burning barrel smoke, marijuana smoke, wildfire smoke,
  firecracker smoke, singed hair smoke
car fire smoke, smoked salmon smoke, dashboard lighter smoke,
  friction-between-two-bodies smoke.

3

At the powwow, my cousin Steve, wearing a red shirt, climbed
  into the camper with a beautiful Indian woman
named Fawn (they were all named Fawn in those days) and
  told me to guard the door.
By the light of the campfire, I peered through the window and
  watched the Indian woman
dip her head into Steve's lap and take him into her mouth.
  I watched Steve lift her head
and kiss her deeply. I wondered how she tasted at that
  exact moment. Then I watched them
both climb into the top bunk. They undressed each other. They
  were shadows moving at new angles.
They became one dark body with impossible limbs. I could not
  see their faces. I could not see
their eyes. I could not see their mouths. I could not see. I added
  more wood to the fire.

4

Because I will be seen in public, my mother sews me
      a ribbon shirt: A black cotton Oxford
with bright red ribbons on the chest and back. I wear
      tight blue jeans. I will wear braids
if I want to attract an Indian woman who speaks
      her tribal language. I will wear
a ponytail if I want to attract an Indian woman
      who plays basketball.
I will wear my hair loose and uncombed if I want
      to attract an Indian woman
who will climb into a camper with me and teach me
      about her dark body.

5

During a break in the powwow, my cousin Steve (you know
      the one) brought a beautiful Indian woman
named Desire back to my house (Her name was Desire.
      This is not a metaphor.) The rest
of my family, my mother and father, my siblings, were still
      at the powwow. "Use my bed,"
I said to Steve and Desire. I listened at the door as Steve
      pulled Desire's panties down
her long, brown legs. I listened at the door as Desire pulled
      the tie from her long, black hair.
I listened at the door as Desire let all of her hair fall back
      to the cool, white sheets.

6

This fancydancer turns cartwheels across the sawdust
      while a dozen Indian women
carefully watch him. He is a stranger at this powwow.
      Nobody knows his name
but his anonymity makes him more handsome. He is tall
      and lanky, his face painted black.
Between songs, he ignores the obvious stares of the
      Indian women and focuses
his attention on the beautiful Indian man in the third row,
      wearing a red shirt.

7

I am married to an Indian woman who wears a red
  quilt when she dances at powwows.
When she is absent, I hold that quilt to my face
  and memorize its smell.

Rise

1

We are taught to take the bread
into our bodies
as proof of Jesus's body.

The bread is metaphor.
The bread is Jesus transubstantiated.
The bread is simply bread.

I have taken all three
of those tenets into my body
though I am Spokane Indian

and also take salmon
into my body
as proof of salmon.

The salmon is my faith returned.
The salmon is not bread
The salmon is simply salmon.

2

Suddenly, we are wed
and I am just as surprised as you
that marriage has become our bread.

You, the Hidatsa Indian
from the North Dakota plains
who did not grow up with salmon

and me, the Spokane, who rarely trusts
the hands of the priest
as he delivers the bread.

During Eucharist, I am afraid
to close my eyes. I want to see
what has been set on the table before me.

Look. I don't know what
would help me believe
that we have become sacred.

Sweetheart, are we the stone
rolling from the mouth
of the tomb that cannot keep him?

Sweetheart, are we the salmon
rising from the mouth
of the river that cannot keep them?

3

If that was Easter
then the church was full
as we stood against the wall

praying for an empty pew.
If that was Easter
then I rose that morning

in love with you
though I rise every morning
from the water, more or less

in love with you.
If that was Easter
then you were asked

to be the Eucharistic minister.
If that was Easter
then you surprised me

by placing salmon on my tongue.
Then I surprised you
by swallowing it whole.

Amen, amen, amen.

The Theology of Cockroaches

Cockroach
Diane says, it might have been
a cockroach
in the upstairs bathroom

though she cannot be positive
because she was otherwise distracted
and only saw it out of the corner
of her eyes, the cockroach

or rather, the potential cockroach
that scuttled along the baseboard
in the bathroom and vanished
before she could get a good look at it.

Have you ever seen a cockroach?
I ask her and she says, Of course
I have, I grew up in California
though I'm not sure what that means

because I've always associated
cockroaches with poverty, grinding
and absolute, constant as gravity
and though I've been poor

I've never been that poor, never
woke to a wall filled with cockroaches
spelling out my name, never
stepped into a dark room and heard

the cockroaches baying at the moon.
Diane saw the cockroach
in the bathroom, one of four bathrooms
in this large house. We are homeowners

and there is a cockroach
or the idea of a cockroach
in the bathroom, a cockroach
scuttling along the hardwood floors.

Did you get a good look at it?
I ask Diane and she says, No, but
it was fast, cockroach-fast.
Not beetle-fast, not

ant-fast, not even spider-fast
but cockroach-fast, disappearing
behind the magazine rack
in the bathroom, slipping

into the crack between floor
and baseboard. Impossible.
Impossible. Impossible.
Impossible. Impossible.

Impossible. The impossible cockroach
is not alone, I think, cockroaches
are never alone, never hermits, never
the last one on the ship, never

the one who dies alone.
Christopher Columbus was a cockroach
and look what followed him.
The cockroach, the cockroach

in the bathroom is watching us
as Diane and I explore
the smallest spaces between
toilet and wall, beneath the sink

and in the drawers that contain
the pieces of our life
together. The cockroach
is watching us as we discuss

our theories
to explain this cockroach:
the neighbors are remodeling
the old house next door, forcing

cockroaches to migrate, perhaps
fleeing from insecticide
and the sudden absence of food.
Maybe it wasn't a cockroach, I say

and Diane agrees. It could have been
any other kind of insect, it
could have been a hummingbird
for that matter, it could have been

an angel sent to test our faith, it
could have been God, God, God.
That cockroach, that angel
scuttles along the hardwood

and Diane sees it out of the corner
of her eye, in her
peripheral vision, and she believes
it was a cockroach

but she cannot be sure, she only
saw it for a brief moment. God
I ask Diane, how many humans have seen
God in person, truly seen God

take shape and form, how many?
Moses saw the Burning Bush, she says.
Moses, Moses, Moses, impossible Moses
scuttling along the hard wood

or was it Pharaoh? Or was the cockroach
on fire? Or was the cockroach
not a cockroach at all, but a visible prayer
a corporeal sin, a tiny piece

of forgiveness? Diane and I kneel
in our bathroom. We are searching
for the cockroach that might have been
a cockroach or nothing at all.

Sugar Town

My father, my Van Gogh, is crazy
from hunger. He cuts off his ear, loses his foot
to the wildfire of diabetes.

"Amputation must be a form of insanity,"
he tells me. "Because I can still feel my foot."
My father, my Van Gogh, is crazy

from absence. He reaches down in his dreams
to scratch the itch of the missing foot
burned to ash in the wildfire of diabetes

then he mixes that ash with blood, the primary
colors thick, nearly stopped with sugar.
My father, my Van Gogh, is crazy

from genius, as he paints, carefully
filling a canvas with row upon row of sugar
cane burning in the wildfire of diabetes,

as farm workers, those brown men, run fearfully
toward the horizon smudged with smoke and sugar.
My father, my Van Gogh, is crazy
from the wildfire of diabetes.

They took his right foot.

He is less

than what
he was.

He will learn to walk again
balanced on a prosthetic foot, braced on a permanent crutch.

He will learn to walk again
if he lives long enough to learn.

That night, as he sleeps
in the recovery room, as he shivers
in the hot room, I kiss him
for the first time in decades. I kiss him

and discover his skin tastes sweet.

Asleep with my infant son, I wake to a noise
somewhere in the dark house. But we are
alone, my son and I, because his mother
my wife, is off to Europe. I have been
frightened in her absence, falling asleep
with my son to make sure he breathes
and of course, he is fine, he continues
to sleep soundly despite my best efforts
to disturb him, as I sit up in bed, in
the dark, and listen, as I hear that noise

again from somewhere inside the house.
I grope around the bed, in hopes of finding
some weapon or something approximating
a weapon. But there is nothing. I am
defenseless there in the dark with my sleeping
son and his mother's absence and the doorway
where a shadow will soon appear, and when
it appears, will it be the Killer of Children, or
the Thief of Babies, or the Saint of Crib Death, or my father

with his feet bloodied from the hundreds of miles
he has walked to come here, now, to tell me
how much he loves me, how much he loves my son?

Before I became a father
I used to stare at women.

Now, I stare at their children.

86

What I mean
is this: We pay
attention to what
is missing
only after it
goes away.

No. Too abstract.

What I mean is this: in moments of great pain
the general becomes particular .

No. Still too abstract.

What I mean is this: When your father loses his foot
you begin to notice other people who have lost their feet.

Of course, I am not
talking about my son
particularly, because he is
innocent. Instead
I will speak of my father
who is guilty of particular sins.

In this dream, the knock
on the front door wakes me

(so I cannot tell if
I am still dreaming
about a knock on the door
or am responding to a true
knock on the door
that has become a part
of my dream)

and I rush downstairs
and fling the door open.

My father's right foot
stands on the welcome mat.

"No," I say to the foot. "You have the wrong house.
I am Sherman Alexie, Junior.
I am the son."

Disappointed, the foot turns
and walks away, though, of course

I wonder how a foot could do anything else
but walk. After all, isn't the act of walking
the foot's sole reason for existence? Step
after step after step, is my father's foot
traveling away from its original mission, its birth
and myth, its creation story?

I carry my father's name
as I will someday carry his coffin.

Before the surgeon took his foot
my father requested an eye patch
a parrot, and a peg leg.

"A pirate," he said, "I'll be a pirate."

Then I knew where I inherited
the inability to remain serious
between and among injuries.

But wait, in my father's defense, in my defense
I must insist that everything is funny.

For instance, before JFK, Jr. flew gently into that good night
in a plane too complicated for him to handle, in weather
that grounded more experienced pilots, on a foot
wrapped in a ten-pound cast, did anybody stop to tell him,
"But John-John, you can't defy death, you're a Kennedy?"

And now, in the middle of all of this, I see my father
riding in the presidential limousine in Dealey Plaza
on November 22, 1963, but he stands on his head
with his bare feet sticking up into the dangerous Texas air.

I love my father
with and without, on
and off, reservations. I want
you to know that.

"But Sherman, you can't defy death, you're an Indian."

Parenthood is no miracle.
There is no magic involved.
There is only the rough sandpaper
of faith, the hard work of love, and it is

work, good and true work, but difficult
as hell. Exhausting. So exhausting, it's easy
for a parent to quit for a second, a minute,
maybe a week, before you remember, regain

the concentration and put your shoulder back
to the wheel, and push, push, push.

Once, when I had not eaten in twenty-four hours
as I waited for my father to come home
from the hunt for money, any money

I prayed for food, for food!
Could that happen
in the United States of America? Yes, I prayed

for food, and just as I whispered, "Amen"
my father walked in the door
with a large bucket of Kentucky Fried Chicken

To all the vegetarians of the world, I say this: FUCK YOU.

In case you were wondering, the chicken was extra crispy.

I am gaining weight as I age. I have my father's jowls.
I fight this but secretly hold out the hope
that I will be a handsome fat man. Now my heart thumps
when I run. I am chasing my father.
I am chasing my father's foot.

Thunder and lightning wakes
my son. I rush
to his room and offer all
the comfort I can give.
My son accepts this. For now
he believes in me
more than he will ever believe
in any god.

That belief in me will change.

But now, in this moment, he quiets.
He inhales, exhales, inhales, exhales.

He sleeps.

In the dark, I hold his small, perfect feet.

I remember when my siblings and I used to hide my father's
    booze
Now we hide the donuts and candy bars.

My earliest memories include a St. Bernard
knocking me off a wood pile, a board game
about the Harlem Globetrotters, a porno movie
at my sister's apartment, and my father's plastic bag
filled with hypodermic needles and insulin bottles.

My oldest brother weighs over four hundred pounds.
My younger sisters, twins, both weigh over two hundred pounds.

Indians dance in circles.

Father, every step I take is a wake.

That cry in the night
is my son, is my father.

Both want me to be
a better man than I am.